Series 536

POND LIFE

by NANCY SCOTT

with illustrations by JILL PAYNE

Publishers: Ladybird Books Ltd . Loughborough
© Ladybird Books Ltd (formerly Wills & Hepworth Ltd) 1966
Printed in England

About Ponds

There are many, many ponds of various kinds for us to explore, even in the heart of our busy towns. Wherever water collects for any length of time, new life springs rapidly into being. You can test this fact for yourself by sinking a bowl into the ground and letting it fill naturally with rainwater. Before many days have passed, you will see that a green scum is beginning to cover the surface. This is called algae, and it has grown from spores so tiny you cannot see them with the naked eye. You need a microscope.

Algae gives off oxygen. All animals need oxygen to live, just as we do; so although this green scum may not look very attractive, it is essential to maintain life in the water.

Watch this new pond, and one day you will see tiny air-bubbles rising to the surface. When this happens you will know for certain that animal life is present.

Now let us part the covering of green scum on the well-established pond in our picture and look at the teeming, bustling life in the water-world below.

Opposite: (*Centre*) *A Water Shrew,* (*top right*) *Yellow Iris,* (*bottom right*) *Purple Loosestrife,* (*bottom centre*) *Water Crowfoot.*

0 7214 0107 4

Water Boatmen

Every stretch of water is covered with a fine skin. This is called the surface-film. It is strong enough to support animals clinging to it below the surface.

In the illustration you can see a Water Boatman clinging to the surface-film. It is having a rest. Nearby is another Water Boatman swimming, but it is swimming on its back! Watch one in a pond and you will see how it uses its hind legs as oars to 'row' itself through the water. Notice the quick, rhythmic way these move, sending its streamlined body swiftly along.

The Water Boatman can fly strongly and moves from pond to pond, so you can be sure of finding it, and its cousin the Lesser Water Boatman, on nearly every pond.

The Lesser Water Boatman spends most of its life at the bottom of the pond—and one is shown swimming towards the plant, Water Soldier. It comes to the surface for a fresh supply of air now and then, so that is when you are most likely to spot one.

Both Boatmen lay their eggs on the water plants.

Water Spiders

There is only one British spider that spends all its life under water, and that is *Argyroneta aquatica*, the Water Spider.

Its brown body is covered with a silvery coat of air-bubbles, and it lives in a house made of air-bubbles, so it will never drown. It collects fresh air-bubbles from the surface as it needs them.

In the summer, when the female Water Spider is ready to lay her eggs, she spins a flat sheet of silk which she attaches to weeds near the surface of the pond. Next she collects many bubbles of air, carrying them down into the pond, and releasing them beneath the silken sheet. As the bubbles rise, they push the middle of the anchored, silken sheet upwards until it is bell-shaped.

The male Water Spider in the picture is shown inspecting the bubble-house which the female has slung between Starwort stems. This silk-roofed bubble-house is divided into two compartments. The upper one is the nursery, the lower one the spider's living room where she keeps guard on her eggs.

The female Water Spider in the picture is chasing a Water Louse. She is smaller than the male, but in most species of spider the female is larger than the male.

Opposite: Plant: *Starwort*.

The Pirate and Raft Spiders

Here are two more spiders which spend much of their life *on* the water, although they do not live right *in* it like the Water Spider. Both are Wolf Spiders, so called because they hunt their food and do not catch it in webs.

The Pirate Spider is well named. Like the marauding pirate of history, it is flamboyant in dress and daring in habit. This one is shown chasing a Dixa Midge across the water, running over the surface-film as easily as it runs over land. And it is no good a midge diving underwater in an effort to escape—the Pirate Spider will dive after it, as it doesn't mind a wetting.

Fiercer still is the Raft Spider. It even has its own 'ship'. In the illustration you can see it perched on a Sycamore leaf floating on the water. It keeps a sharp watch out, and the moment it sees a tasty insect to its liking, away it goes, captures the prize and brings it back aboard. There it enjoys its meal in comfort.

Opposite: Plants: *Duckweed and Sycamore leaf.*

The Silver Water Beetle
and Great Diving Beetle

All the different kinds of water beetles have a similar life history—first the egg, then larva, pupa and finally the adult winged insect.

Notice the silvery sheen covering the under-surface of the large water beetle on the right of our picture. This is caused by the supply of air it carries about with it. The bubbles are trapped among the body hairs. Nearly all the adult Silver Water Beetles are vegetarians, but the larvae, which hatch out of the egg cocoons to be found floating on the surface of the water, are carnivorous. They particularly like small water snails.

The adult Great Diving Beetle on the left is a fierce insect, and is carnivorous. It not only eats other pond insects, but also pond snails, tadpoles, small fishes, and even its own kind.

The female Great Diving Beetle lays her eggs inside the stems of water plants in the spring. That strange-looking creature shown clinging to the Hornwort is the larva. It has to cling like this as its body is lighter than water, and when it lets go, it automatically floats to the surface.

When fully-grown, the larva of both the Silver Water Beetle and the Great Diving Beetle leaves the pond and hollows out a tiny den in some damp earth nearby. Hidden in its den, it moults and changes to the pupa stage. It may stay in this stage for only a few weeks, or sometimes for the whole winter.

The adults hibernate in the mud at the bottom of the pond all the winter.

Opposite: Plant: *Hornwort with larva attached.*

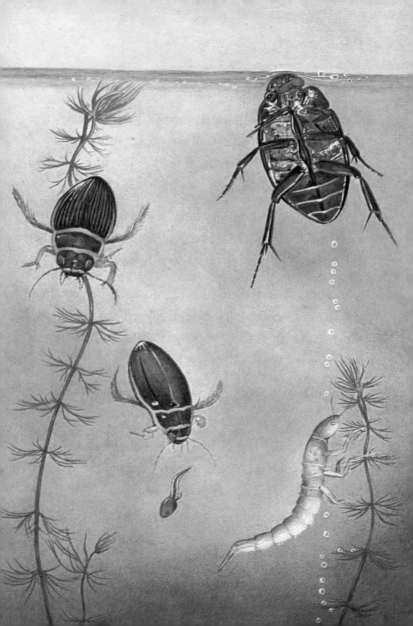

Pond Snails

You will see snails crawling over the weeds under-water. The Ram's Horn shell in the centre of our picture is the species kept in aquariums to keep the glass free from algae. All snails feed on algae, using an organ called a radula to rasp it off the surface of plants and stones.

This radula is like a very long, coiled tongue equipped with rows and rows of teeth. As the teeth wear out they are replaced by the band growing forward.

The big snail hanging upside down is the common Great Pond-snail. It is clinging to a band of its own slime which in turn is attached to the surface-film of the water.

At the bottom of the pond you can see the Wandering Snail.

All the snails lay their eggs in gelatinous capsules, attached to plants. You can see the eggs of the Wandering Snail on the Fennel-leaved Pondweed to the left of our picture.

Opposite: Plant: *Fennel-leaved Pondweed with snail's eggs attached.*

Freshwater Mussels and Cockles

To look closely at freshwater mussels and cockles you may need a hand net. Drag it carefully along the muddy bottom of a pond, and you will bring up several interesting species.

The Swan Mussel not only likes to hide at the bottom of the pond, but also keeps very still and this makes it even more difficult to spot. When it does need to move, it does so very slowly indeed, as it has only one muscular foot with which to propel itself along.

It lays thousands of eggs during the summer, and keeps them in special brood pouches in the outer gills. They stay there for about nine months, then each larva that has developed escapes and holds on to water-weeds by fine silken threads.

The next stage in the life of a larva is very strange. As a fish swims by, the larva becomes attached to its skin. It burrows into the skin, a protective covering forms over it, and in this it gradually develops into a miniature Swan Mussel. This takes about three months, and during that time it feeds on its host, so it is a parasite for this stage of its life.

The smaller shells are Orb-Shell Cockles. They are more active and can climb the stems of water-weeds.

Opposite: Plant: *Curled Pondweed.*

The Rat-tailed Maggot and the Hover Fly

In the illustration the maggot shown with its own snorkel is the larva of a Hover Fly. It is called the Rat-tailed Maggot, and you will find it in shallow ponds, or in the shallow edges of deeper ponds.

The last segment of its body is stretched out into a very long tail. This tail is in three segments which can be telescoped into one another, or can be extended if the water gets deeper. Right at the tip of this long snorkel-tube is a tuft of tiny, feathery hairs, and it is these the Rat-tailed Maggot pokes up out of the water, because in the centre of them are the air passages through which it breathes.

It can move about freely on the bottom of the pond, using the seven pairs of hooked foot warts you can see under its plump body.

Its skin hardens when it is ready to pupate, and inside this hard case the fly forms. When it crawls out it will look like that plump fly hovering over the water's edge. It looks like a bee, but that is camouflage, as it is really a fly. Notice that it has only *one* pair of wings. A bee has two pairs.

The floating water plant on the left is Frogbit. During the summer months it produces small white flowers which have only three petals.

Opposite: Plants: (*left*) *Frogbit* and (*right*) *flowering and seeding Flowering Rush.*

Gnats

The Gnats around a pond are a nuisance on a warm, damp day, but you will find their life history very interesting.

The mouth of the female is specially adapted to prick your skin, then suck your blood. It is only the female who sucks blood, and she needs to do so to enable her eggs to mature. As she sucks she injects juices which cause the swelling that irritates so much.

Among that swarm above the pond are many females ready to lay. They lay their eggs in groups of two hundred to three hundred in tiny egg-rafts. There is one shown floating on the surface, towards the left of the picture. Just below the surface, to the right, you can see some eggs that have already hatched out. The larvae live in this surface layer of water, hanging head downwards. At this stage they breathe through a tube in the abdomen. But when they pupate they turn the other way up, because now they breathe through two little tubes on the head and thorax, and with these they attach themselves to the surface-film. There is one on the far left of the picture, just below the sedge.

Opposite: Plants (*left*) Sedges and (*below water*) Canadian Pondweed.

Water Skaters

Here are two insects you can watch on the surface of the pond. The thin-bodied ones at the bottom of the picture are so light that they can walk over the surface of the water without breaking through the surface-film. These are Water Measurers.

Look closely at one of these small, wingless insects and you will see that it has a long, peculiarly shaped head with the eyes set low down in the narrowest part.

The larger insects are the Pond Skaters. The Water Measurer walks slowly over the surface of the water, giving you time to examine it properly, but the Pond Skater is much quicker in its movements. It seems to slide over the surface of the pond, sometimes giving quite long jumps in comparison with its size.

The Skater and the Measurer are both covered in a thick coat of fine hairs, which is particularly thick on the underside. This coat holds air and so keeps them dry, and safe from drowning.

Some species of Pond Skaters have normal wings, some have short wings, and some have no wings at all, so it is very difficult to tell a fully-formed adult from a nymph.

Opposite: Plants (*above*) Ivy-leaved Duck-weed, (*below*) Lesser Duckweed.

Water Plants

Plants that grow in the water have to be specially fitted for living in a permanently liquid home. These beautiful Water-lilies are good examples. Their leaf-stalks are so long, and the leaves so large and heavy, that they could not support themselves in the air. But in the water the leaves float easily.

When the seeds of the Water-lily are ready for dispersal, they float away from the parent plant, each one surrounded and supported on the water by a mass of tiny air-bubbles. When the bubbles burst, the seed sinks to the bottom of the pond and starts a new plant.

In flowing water, many of the pond plants have two different kinds of leaves. The upper ones, floating on the surface, are large and flat; but the leaves below the water look like long green ribbons. These narrow leaves offer less resistance to the current, so there is no danger that when the water flows more quickly the plant will be torn up by the roots.

The Water-crowfoot shown below the Water-lilies, and the Arrowhead to the left of the picture both have two different types of leaves.

Opposite: Plants (*on water*) *Water Lilies* and (*nearer*) *Water Crowfoot*, (*left*) *Arrowhead and Common Reeds.*

The Moorhen and Wagtail

Did you notice that bird walking across the lily leaves on the previous page? That was a Pied Wagtail. You will see many near ponds, constantly flicking their tails and looking for pond insects.

Now look among the Rushes and Water Plantain in the picture opposite, and you will see a grass-lined, reedy Moorhen's nest. It does not belong to that family of Moorhens swimming so happily among the tiny Duckweed and Broad-leaved Pondweed, because the large clutch of eggs has not yet hatched out.

The Moorhen occurs abundantly throughout the British Isles, and can even be found on water in the heart of London. It eats insects, worms, slugs, water vegetation and some grain. At breeding time the male birds fight grimly for the females' favour.

Moorhens are excellent swimmers, both on and under the water; but they are excellent walkers, too, and have very long, unwebbed toes.

You might, at first, confuse the Moorhen with the Coot, another water bird. You can tell the difference as the Coot is bigger and has a *white* patch on the front of its head.

Opposite: Plants (*foreground*) *Rushes*, (*left*) *Broad-leaved Pondweed*, (*right*) *Water Plantain*.

Frogs and Toads

Another animal you may see on the wide, thick leaves of the Water-lily is the Frog.

That mass of black-speckled jelly shown on top of the water is frog spawn, and each one of those specks is an egg. In the water below, you can see the tadpoles that have already hatched from some of the eggs. The tadpole is the next stage of development, and although the frog can live quite well on land, the tadpole cannot. At this stage of its life, the tiny tadpole has no lungs, only gills—like fishes—so it would suffocate if it tried to follow its parents on to the bank of the pond.

As you will see, some of the tadpoles have no legs at all, just a body and a tail—they are the newly-hatched ones. Some have one pair of legs near the base of the tail—they are just over two months old. Those with two pairs of legs, and the tail getting smaller and smaller are almost fully-formed frogs, and as soon as they develop lungs they will be able to leave the water.

Toads also lay their eggs in water and develop in much the same way as the frogs, but the toad spawn is laid in long strips attached to and wound round water-weeds. You can see some curled round the Canadian Pondweed and Reeds to the right of the picture, above the Water Moss.

Opposite: Plants (*below*) *Water Moss*, (*centre*) *Canadian Pondweed with Reeds at sides.*

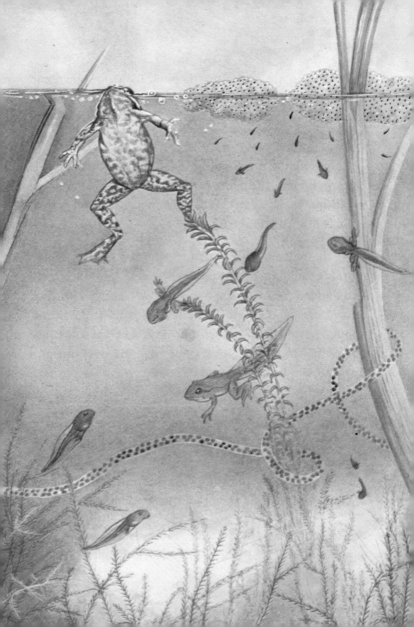

Newts

When you are exploring the pond for frog spawn and tadpoles, you may see some other tiny creatures rather like tadpoles, but slimmer and with longer tails. These are Newt larvae.

In our picture are a male and female Smooth Newt. It is springtime, so the male (at the top) is wearing his courting attire, a wavy crest. When the mating season is over he will lose this fine frill.

At the bottom of the picture you can see two leaves of the Canadian Pondweed bent over. Look closely and hidden below each one you will be able to pick out an egg of the newt. The female is most particular about the places in which she lays her eggs because unlike the frog, she lays very few eggs and only one at a time, so she has to choose the safest possible position for them.

Newt larvae take much longer to grow than frog tadpoles, so you can find them in the pond all the summer. Usually they are fully-formed newts by the autumn, but sometimes they are very slow in developing and so remain in the ponds as larvae all the winter.

You can see the size of these Newts when you compare them with the Ram's-Horn Snail.

The Water Vole and Water Shrew

As you walk quietly up to the edge of a pond, you are almost certain to hear a sudden, loud plop. This will probably be a Water Vole diving into the water. Even though you walk on tip-toe, it will still hear you, because the Vole has very keen hearing. However, its eyesight is poor, so if you can sit absolutely still for a while it will soon come out of the water and on to the bank again.

You know how a Squirrel sits up on its haunches to eat a nut? The Water Vole nibbles at a piece of waterweed or willow bark in just the same way, as you can see in the illustration.

The female Water Vole makes a thick-walled, round nest of reeds and grasses in a special chamber in one of the many burrows under the bank. In this she usually gives birth to about five tiny, naked, blind babies. She will probably have three more families like this during the summer months.

That tiny, silvery-coated animal shown swimming in the water isn't a small Water Vole. It is a Water Shrew. Notice its longer snout. The Water Shrew also tunnels and nests in the banks. It is a wonderful swimmer and as it rarely goes far from the bank, you will be able to watch its aquatic abilities for as long as you can keep still enough not to be heard.

Whirligig Beetles

Favourite food of the Voles and Shrews is the restless Whirligig Beetle. You will see colonies of them swimming fantastically fast round and round in circles and spirals on the surface of the water. Their middle and hind legs are wide and flat, and have long swimming hairs on them which make them perfect for rapid swimming movements.

Because the Whirligig Beetle lives on the surface of the water, it has enemies above *and* below, so to help it escape it has a special adaptation to its eyes. Each compound eye is divided into two across the centre, giving it an upper and a lower half. With the upper part it can see above the surface, and with the lower part it can see below the surface. So, in effect, it has two pairs of eyes.

If you put your finger near one, it will disappear rapidly below the surface, carrying an air-bubble with it.

The eggs and the larvae live in the water until late July, then the larvae climb up water plants and each one spins for itself a cocoon above the water level. But you will be very fortunate if you find one of these cocoons, as they are always very well hidden.

Opposite: Plants: *Reeds and Water Plantain.*

China Mark Moths

You would not usually expect to find a moth caterpillar living in the water, yet the caterpillars of the China Mark Moths live a fully aquatic life.

The Beautiful China Mark, shown on the left, and the Brown China Mark, on the right, both lay their eggs mainly on the Bur-reed. When the eggs hatch out, the caterpillars feed on the plant, and to protect themselves they each make a floating case of the Bur-reed leaves, by binding together bitten-off pieces with fine silk made from their own bodies.

Inside this portable covering the caterpillar lives from about midsummer until the next spring. It breathes through its skin and at first this skin is easily wetted; but after several moults the skin becomes covered with hairs which makes the surface of its body unwettable. When this happens the caterpillar is surrounded by air in its case.

In the following spring, the caterpillar is ready to pupate, so it fixes its case to a water-plant with silk, and closes both ends securely. In June or July the adult moths emerge; so the whole life-cycle of the various China Mark Moths takes about a year.

Opposite: Plant: *Bur-reed*.

Dragonfly Nymphs

Down in the depths of the pond, almost hidden by the mud and plants at the bottom, lives one of the greatest tyrants of the underwater world. This is the larva, usually called a nymph, of the Dragonfly.

It is carnivorous, that is, it feeds on other animals. You can see how the one in the picture is lurking among the weeds. This is a half-grown Emperor nymph, and it is waiting for one of those tiny tadpoles to swim near enough to be seized. To do this, it will use a peculiar organ popularly called a mask. This is a long apparatus with strong hooks on the end, and which is normally kept folded away below the nymph's head. When its chosen prey swims near, out shoots this mask, hooks the victim and pulls it backwards towards the nymph's mouth.

There are many species of dragonfly nymph; some live in the pond for only a few months, others for perhaps three or four years. This particular nymph will live among these water-weeds for one year, and during that time it will change its skin many times as it grows. At about the fifth or sixth moult the wings will begin to form, because these nymphs do not go through a pupal stage.

Climbing up the stem of Mare's-tail is a fully-grown nymph. It is ready to undergo its final moult. Let us follow it and see what happens.

Opposite: Plants *(below) Water Moss, (left) Mare's Tail, (right) Water Crowfoot.*

Dragonflies

Now you can see the beautiful creature that under-water tyrant has become—a handsome Emperor Dragon-fly. A male Emperor is shown on the bottom right of the picture. The skin of the ugly nymph splits across the back for the last time, and this beautiful insect pushes its way out of its old casing.

While it is waiting for its skin to burst open, the nymph clings exceedingly tightly to the weed. Because of this, the larval skin remains attached to the plant for a long time after the dragonfly has flown away, so you should be able to find some empty cases to examine. Also it may take a dragonfly several hours to emerge from its larval skin, and gain strength, so there is a very good chance you will see this wonderful transformation for yourself one day.

When this lovely Emperor gains its full strength, it flies away to join the other dragonflies, and find a mate. Watch it flying. It is extremely skilful in flight. It can hover, and even fly backwards when it wishes. Notice also how it can move both pairs of wings alternately, so giving it greater power in flight.

The other dragonflies in the picture are: top left, Cordulegaster boltonii (male); bottom left, a Damoiselle Angrion Virgo (male); top right, Libellula depressa (female).

Opposite: Plants: (*below*) *Flowering Rushes*, (*top*) *Willow leaves*.

Mallards

You might think that there are two different species of duck shown in this picture but this is not so. The handsomely marked bird is a Mallard drake, and the other bird is the hen, his mate. Mallards mate for life.

Their nest is well hidden in the vegetation at the pond-edge. It is made of grass and dead leaves, and lined with dark brown down plucked from the breast of the mother duck. When she wants to leave the nest for a while, she will hide the eggs by covering them with some of this down.

The chicks can swim from the moment they hatch out of the eggs. They are covered with brown and buff streaked hair, long and downy, and have a distinctive dark eye-stripe. This eye-stripe will help you identify young Mallards, as they do not develop their adult plumage until after their first winter.

If the chicks are alarmed when swimming, they at once dive below the surface, leaving just their tiny heads out of the water. You will then need very sharp eye-sight to see them.

Opposite: Plant: *Flowers of Flowering Rush.*

Willows

Trees and shrubs growing around the pond are very important to the life within and by the water. Their roots bind the earthy banks together and prevent them being washed away; their branches and leaves give shade in summer, and their continual growth forms a necessary food-supply for the insects and other creatures.

The most familiar waterside trees are willows. There are many different kinds, but examine the leaves and you will soon be able to tell one from the other.

The handsome silvery-looking tree is the White Willow. On the far side of the pond you can see an older willow which has been pollarded, that is, the shoots have been cut back every year or so to prevent the tree growing too tall and cumbersome.

To the right are the green branches of the Crack Willow. Bend a twig of this willow and it will break off with a sharp crack; that is how it got its popular name. None of the other willow twigs do this.

At the bottom of the picture are two sprays of Osier. On the left the Common Osier and on the right the Purple Osier.

Two other small shrubs you may find will be Goat-willow and Common Sallow. These give you the beautiful golden catkins gathered as 'palm' for decorating our churches on Palm Sunday.

The Minnow, Gudgeon, Stone Loach
and Bullhead

Did you know that Minnows are very inquisitive? Anything unusual, in addition to food, dropping on to the surface of the water will arouse their curiosity at once, and bring a large shoal to gather round and stare inquiringly from all sides.

It is this curiosity which gives us such a wonderful chance to watch these pretty little fish. Most of the fish, like the Gudgeon just below the minnows, the Stone Loach on the bottom left and the Bullhead on the right, prefer to stay on or near the bottom of the water, hiding among the stones and weeds.

Sometimes a pond will dry up if we have a hot summer. When this happens, the Stone Loach buries itself in the soft mud and lives there in a torpid condition until the rains fill the pond again.

At breeding time the Bullheads scoop out a little hollow beneath a stone. The eggs are stuck to the stone and stay there until the young hatch out and swim away. While they are hatching, the male Bullhead is a most conscientious father, guarding them day and night.

When a Bullhead is caught and kept in an aquarium, you can hear the strange creaking sound it makes when moving its gill-covers. The popular name for the fresh-water Bullhead is Miller's Thumb, because its flat head is said to be like the flattened thumb of a miller.

Opposite: Plant: *Millfoil*.

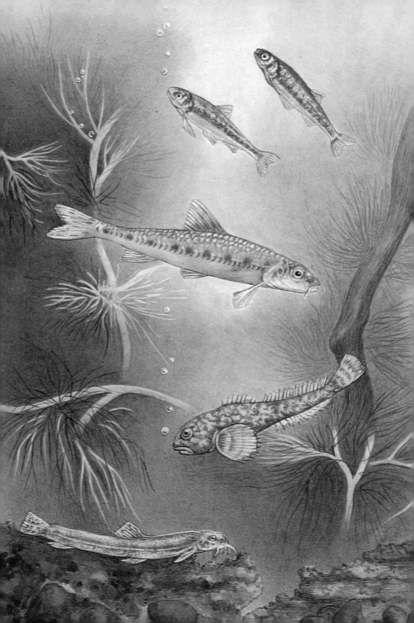

Common Water-fleas, Daphnia, Cyclops and Hydra

Scoop up a handful of water from any pond and you will be holding in your palm dozens and dozens of minute live animals. Many of them can only be seen through the lens of a microscope, but others can be seen with the naked eye if you look closely, or better still, with a simple hand lens.

Shown on the right, above the weeds, are some Common Water-fleas, so called because they move through the water with a series of hops or jumps. Daphnia, another species of water-flea, is nearby. You can see that its body is rounder and it has a tail-like spine.

You will be able to spot a female Cyclops, without a lens, if she is carrying her egg sacs as in the middle of our picture. But you will need your lens to pick out the young Cyclops which hatch out of the eggs. They are no bigger than tiny pencil dots.

Attached to the weed is a green specie of Hydra. This animal holds fast to the plants with the aid of a sucking disc. At the other end, among the hair-like tentacles, is its mouth. The tiny branches near its base are new Hydras growing. They soon become detached and live a separate life from the parent animal. This method of reproduction is called 'budding'. But at certain times of the year, Hydras also produce a tiny egg which, at a certain stage, is released into the water.

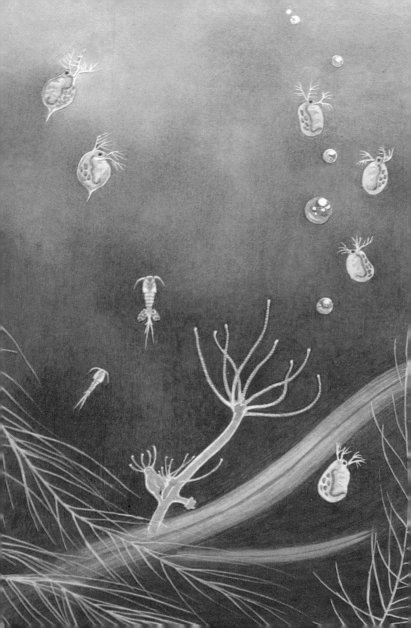

Surrounding Plants

Around the edges of our ponds you will always find plants which like to have their roots well set in wet, muddy soil. One of the first of these to flower is the Marsh Marigold, or Kingcup.

The Marsh Marigold has no petals. Watch the buds opening and you will see that the *sepals* gradually deepen in tone to a beautiful, golden yellow—these take the place of the petals and attract the insects to the nectar.

Butterbur is another early flowering, waterside plant. Usually the flowers appear before the leaves, but if you find the flowers early in the spring, then be sure to visit the pond again later in the summer to see how enormous its leaves have grown. They will look like giant Rhubarb leaves, and many people call them Wild Rhubarb.

The first flowers of the Water Forget-me-not are shown only just open. Like the Marsh Marigold, many of them pass through an interesting colour-change. At first the youngest flowers are often a delicate pink, with no trace of blue.

Many more flowers come into bloom around the edges of a pond as the months go by. Among them may be Yellow Iris, creamy-white Meadowsweet, red Hemp Agrimony, Purple Loosestrife, blue Skullcap and the mauve Greater Willow-Herb—to name only a few.

Opposite: Plants: (*Centre left*) *Marsh Marigolds*, (*centre right*) *Amphibious Persicaria*, (*bottom*) *Water Forget-me-not*, (*at top*) *Willow branch*.